Preface

*Immortalized
In what we write
All we scribe
Is meant to rise
A nation of people
Thinkers and healers
Feel what we're feeling
A part of history
Generational healing*

Contents of A Revolution
- Righteous Hands.....5
- Regularly Scheduled Programming.....9
- America The Beautiful.....10
- Poetic Justice.....14
- Pay.....16
- Us.....18
- Payed Attention.....30
- Take A Penny, Take A Penny.....33
- United States..... 39
- Niggers.....42
- Black Lives.....48
- Ripped Van's Winkle.....58
- A King's Fantasy.....61
- MicroAggression.....65
- Comply 'Til We Die.....68
- Mason Bricking.....71
- Oak to Mahogany.....74
- Watered Seeds.....76
- Society Has Forsaken The Black Father.....80
- Unlearn/Relearn.....90
- Us in Black Skin.....94
- Tree of Life.....96
- Legacy.....108
- Perspectives.....114
- Prophet/NonProphet.....115
- Numbers Do Know Boundaries.....117
- Bored in Sin.....122
- Black Wombman Is GOD.....124
- Pharm to Market Road.....129
- Soapbox.....132
- Acknowledgements.....137
- About the Author.....138

Janeé Vaughn Presents Book One of Jasmine's Twilight: Twilight of a Revolution:

A Collection of Poetry
Published by JasminesTwilight
Bedford, Texas

All rights reserved. No part of this publication may be reproduced, stored in a retrieval system, or transmitted, in any form or by any means, electronic, mechanical, photocopying, recording, or otherwise, without written permission of the publisher.

ISBN: 978-0-578-77198-4
LCCN: 2021915391
Printed in The United States of America

Thank you for supporting the Twilight of a Revolution!

Janeé

TRIBE NUBIAN Writers

Righteous Hands

Righteous hands cover palms
On Sundays spent on lawns
Watching Pick Niccs,
Feasting on the flesh
Of the body of a Christ with no father.

Belles in bonnets of blue,
Children's laughter while dandelion seeds
float through,
Blankets splayed out to watch the show,
Parents keeping eyes on children,
As to the bottoms of hills they wander below.
Sun is setting on front porch gallows, while
brewing peach tea.
The wind is blowing the scent of jasper leaves.

Men gathered in mob style fashion,
To fashion their showstopper
With a neck-tied fastening.
And herein stands,
Future dearly departed,
Still searching for a pardon
Of sins uncommitted.

Death sentence for living,
Existing...
Breathing...
In spaces deemed unworthy
For hued men, women, & children
of a 'lesser' god.
Beaten, eaten, flogged

By righteous hands
What cover palms,
On Sundays spent on lawns,
Watching Pick Niccs,
Feasting on the flesh
Of the body of a Christ with no father.

His children unallowed to play on those hills
It's forbidden.
Only allowed to serve their father's storyline villains.
Serving the Masters,
Masticating on burnt toes to ribs shred by the crowd.
Both jeers and cheers shouted out loud.
While in the barnyard entrenched behind arenas abound

*Mary Magdalen's loins are purloined like loot
for fodder by unwanted suitors.
Suited in the blood of a Christ
They choose to chew on.
Sun setting with the cinders still hot to the
touch.
Mary Magdalen's skin: raw from the influx.*

*Children are simmering down.
Women are calling all home.
Yet. a Christ with no father
Has children who must roam
In the swamps in the dead of night
Sneaking by while their mother goes through
her trials
A father's sacrifice and a mother's burden
To save their future generations from
hurting
Only to live again
In this same cycle of sin.
Mother named whore
Touched and unadorned by*

*Righteous hands what cover palms
On Sundays spent on lawns*

Watching Pick Niccs,
Feasting on the flesh
Of the body of a Christ with no father.

Fatherless homes; still burdens of mothers.
Separation of families is the cross of our brothers,
Who turn into a Christ with no father,
Persecuted by those same tombed crosses
From roads they've been running.
Crowned victorious
On set stages
At the crossroads they have to choose to travel daily.
Death Valley in a crown of thorns,
Bleeding minds and hearts
Flowing onto palms of righteous hands
Shaming their own brethren.

While they spend Sundays
Sitting as pawns
Watching Pick Niccs,
Feasting on the flesh
Of the body of a Christ with no father.
We are Christ's lost children.

Regularly Scheduled Programming

What did they do to a black woman,
to make her think
this is the way,
twerking on a pole
just to get some bread?
Easy answer.
They pried the black man away.
Now the black man's pride
won't allow him to educate
himself enough
to be what she needs.
She's out here dropping that thang
while she's carrying his seeds,
Even if he protests
it's a woman's choice now
All he can do is concede
feminism is our devil
Was never our cause
now all she doin'
is droppin' it low
And droppin' her drawls
black men
make a mockery of us daily
yet we don't take as much
As a pause to see
that we were set up
on self-destruct mode,
we hold the TNT
shameful,
to parade our own disgraces
I mean, you don't see that
in all these other "races" ...
But the black American
so proud and
unfree
Man!
damn the black American,
defunct of unity

AMERICA THE BEAUTIFUL

AMERICA THE BEAUTIFUL?
HOME OF HOLLYWOOD
STARS PROMOTE THE
DEATH OF SOCIETY
GOVERNMENT CONTROLS
OUR DIET
PATENTS ON WIND
AND THE SEEDS THEY
CARRY
GMO VEGGIES, MEATS,
JUICES, & BERRIES
POLICE ARE AT WAR
WITH THE PEOPLE AT LARGE
MAJORITY IS MINORITY
TIME TO TAKE A STAND
REALIZE WE HOLD THE CARDS
WE GOT THE UPPER HAND

FEED YOUR SOUL, YOUR SPIRIT
WITH KNOWLEDGE TO CLAIM
YOUR GROUND
CHALLENGE THEIR ACTIONS
WITH ACTIONS
THAT DON'T MAKE A SOUND
RIOTS, LOOTING, KILLING
THAT'S WHAT THEY EXPECT
CHALLENGE YOURSELF AND
GIVE EM SOMETHING THEY'LL REGRET

KNOWLEDGE IS POWER
MEDIA IS WEAK
DON'T FALL FOR THE
SUBLIMINAL MESSAGES
BE FREE TO BE A FREAK
STRONG BODY & A STRONGER
MIND
LET THE TRUTH BE
EASY TO FIND
SHARE THE WEALTH OF KNOWLEDGE
NOT THIS VIRAL YOUTUBE NONSENSE

Poetic Justice

Poetic justice
that makes that poet a suspect.
From pulpits to court rooms
that's got that poet on judgment.
That flow get 'em gasping and clutching.
Yeah, that whole room it be bumping.
This poet came up
to serve some poetic justice.

Justice, you wanna know what that is?
We talk about fake asses that's plump
and lace fronts,
forget about the guns they take from us.
Forget slavery
they still rapin' us.
Forget the time we spend
chasing that shmoney bus.
Forget that we've BEEN here
still treated like a guest.
forget
that we never knew real JUSTICE.

Under this racist reign,
all we feel is generational pain,
our families ripped apart.
We no longer have a hearth.
It's no longer about us
It's all about the game
Yet, we call out for justice.
Results still the same.

Jasmine's Twilight

Wearing white faces to try and blend in...
Accepting that one dude,
who has that one black best friend.
Watching our women and men
slaughtered every day.
Watching our babies torn apart,
that hit a nigger baby display,
that gator bait,
that juvenile court room
that says he's an adult at 8.
And we're still drinking Starbucks
like everything's just fine.
Still rocking blood diamonds
Hollerin' 'bout how we shinin'.
Still wearing Gucci 'n Louis
An' all these other designers.
Still drinking waters stolen by Nestlé
And Arizona Iced Teas.
Cops patrol you freeze.
Yet, you run up on me,
while Jamal down the block
just sitting with his baby's mom
got run up on and shot,
no less by the cops.
Or ya boy Ju Ju they wanna free.
15 years charges on some weed.
And now,
that's how they get their money!
Yet, justice we call,
forgetting there's no justice for us.
There's no justice at all

until we stand up,
for that

Poetic justice
that makes that poet a suspect.
From pulpits to court rooms
that's got that poet on judgment.
That flow get 'em gasping and clutching.
Yeah, that whole room it be bumping.
Thank you for reading
my poetic justice.

Pay

To seal with pitch or tar to prevent leakage
Payed themselves in sunbath sessions
Payed gram for gram
High dollars for melanin
Payed semen to seep in genes
Payed our babies' spiritual essence
As they hang 'til they bleed
While they clamor at their screams
Tarred in our tar to pay their seams
Loose cannon genes
To lay dormant
Pay to silence their X Warriors
Lineage delineation inevitable

Ain't no amount of melanin
Gonna stable unstable
Yet, they take uteruses
While we lay awake on tables
Still, they take unbaked babies
To add to their periodic tables
Still, they take our young ones
To serve at their dinner tables
Still our stillbirths
Are a dish served cold
Like this injustice idea
America stole
Imperialist capitalists
Still payed toles
Hanging on mantles
Passed downed stories told
Sequined sequence
To pay their way
Delinquent lineage
Changing history
Pay by pay

Janee Vaughn, *Tired*, July 24, 2020, illustration

US
BLACK SKINNED
LIVING IN OUR LAST JUDGMENT
WE BE BROKEN HOME
STREET WALKING
SINNER
TARGET RANGE SHOOT
GRADUATION. HE'S JUST
A BEGINNER
ANOTHER WHITE
HAT IN BROWN SKIN
ON THE LOOSE
ALL YOU SEE IS
HATE PASSED DOWN
DOWN SOUTH DEEP ROOTS
DUG OURSELVES INTO
OUR OWN GRAVES
PLOT TWIST IS
THAT'S HOW THEY
WANT US TO BEHAVE

THEY WANT US
TO REMAIN
MENTAL SLAVES
BUT WHEN IT
COMES TO THIS NATION
WE ARE THE FOUNDATION
BECAUSE WE ARE
WHO THEY FOUND
WHEN THEY
DECIDED TO
FOUND THIS NATION
REALITY IS WE
HAVE MORE SOLID MARRIAGES
REALITY IS WE
HAVE LESS DRUG
EPIDEMICS
REALITY IS WE HAVE
LESS HOMELESSNESS
WE HOLD US ACCOUNTABLE
WE GOT US

Jasmine's Twilight

SO THEY TAKE US
REMODEL REMAKE US
BOBBY BROWN GUMBY
CLAY MATE US
CELL BLOCK TO CELL BLOCK
BETWEEN MUSLIM AND
ARYAN NATION
SO WE CAN DEBATE US
USING GLORIFIED
SWITCH BAIT TACTICS
BUT THEY CAN'T FIT
OUR SHOES
SO THEY FASHION US
IN THEIR IDEA OF FASHION
THEN FASHION US IN
A NOOSE
FORGET THAT WE ARE
THE NEWS

Jasmine's Twilight

DNA WON'T
LET US LOSE
SO THEY PULL
TIGHTER ON THAT
NOOSE
CHOKING ON THAT PICTURE
BROADCAST ON THE NEWS
MUSIC VIDEO, MOVIE
FILM PROJECTION
THEIR PROJECTIONS
OF OUR SELF IMAGES
DRUG ADDICTS,
HIP HOP ACTORS,
UNTALENTED MUMBLE RAPPERS
FAKE FINANCIAL STATISTICS
PROPAGATING
SINGLE, ANGRY
BLACK WOMAN VISUALS

Jasmine's Twilight

TO SELL US THE
IDEA THAT WE ARE
WORTH LESS THAN
OUR OWN MELANIN
GRAM FOR GRAM
IT'S ENOUGH TO
TIP THE SCALE AGAINST
STOCK MARKET CRASH
WHILE BLACK
MARKETS STAY
STABLE
SO ORGANS OF BLACK
BABIES, BLACK
UTERUSES, AND BLACK
STEM CELLS
LAY ON COLD TABLES
WEIGHT OF OUR
WEIGHT IN GRAMS
KEEPS THEIR
BODIES STABLE

ECONOMICALLY, GRAM
FOR GRAM WE RAISE
THEIR PORTFOLIO
STOCK MARKET TABLES
CAPITALISM IS A
GAME THAT WASN'T
MADE FOR US
THEIR MONOPOLY'S
AROUND THE BOARD
INCLUDING THE
BOARDWALK
JAILBAIT THAT'S
STILL US ON
EVERY CORNER OF
THE GAME
MONEY HUNGRY
LANDLORDS TAXING US
JUST TO STAY
IN OUR OWN LANE

GOVERNMENT CORRUPTION
GAVE US THE BLUES
FROM SLAVE CATCHER
TO NYPD, NOPD &
ORANGE COUNTY HUES
CARTING US OFF IN
WAGONS
STICKING US WITH
VICTIMED IDENTITIES
LOSING THE RIGHT
TO CHOOSE
SLAVING US IN THIS
INDUSTRIAL JUDICIARY
TO SURVIVE WE SING
THE BLUES
OF SNITCH, SNITCH,
SNITCH, SNITCH, GOOSE
AND IT'S A TIGHTER
HOLD ON THIS NOOSE

SUFFOCATING US IN OUR OWN
INABILITY TO BREATHE FOR
A MOMENT
ATTACK AFTER ATTACK
THEY WON'T LET UP ON US
LINE AFTER LINE OF OUR
ANCESTOR'S PROTECTION
WON'T STOP THE GAME
THEY HAVE IN STORE
FOR US

Jasmine's Twilight

US
AT RED LIGHTS,
STOP SIGNS, AND
CORNER STORES
GROCERY AISLES, NAIL
SHOPS, & SCHOOL CORRIDORS
((SCHOOL CORRIDORS))
((SCHOOL CORRIDORS))
STRIP SEARCHED FOR VIOLATIONS
UN-MIRANDIZED OF OUR
RIGHTS
BY LAW WE HOLD A
DIFFERENT STATION
SO, IT'S TO THE
STATION THEY TAKE
US
PLANT CHARGES AND
FINE CHINA DUST
IN CAR CONSOLES
AND JACKETS TUCKED

ALL CAUGHT ON CAMERA
THAT'S STILL CLOSED
CAPTIONED TO US
BROADCASTING FOR LAUGHTER
AND A TALLY OF US
COURTROOM JUSTICE SCALES
STILL WEIGH UNJUST
TWENTY YEARS TO LIFE
OR OUR LIFE TAKEN
FROM US
ON A TRAFFIC STOP
FOR SMOKING A CIGARETTE
OR SELLING A COUPLE
LOOSIES
OR JUST SHOWING UP
BLACK THAT DAY
NO REASON FOR THEIR
RULING

RULING: GUILTY VERDICT
NO COURT CAN SUPERCEDE IT
ANOTHER LIFE TAKEN
ANOTHER IDENTITY, OR
MISS TAKEN
UNJUSTLY CAUSE
LIVING IN OUR LAST JUDGMENT
THAT BLACK SKIN
THAT BLACK SKIN
THAT BLACK SKIN
THAT BE US

Payed Attention

We be
Venetian coins
They be
Tarnishing our copper tones
into drones of less supremacy
Lest we forget
We be
Beings of heroic royalty
Sequins of armor
Subjected to jester rulings
Sequence they harm
Warrior X makings
Trying to be baked in
To still sequential matters
Non cents of our skin
Auto pilot to be hung by juries
Persecution's martyrs
Caught up in political parties

Never made for us
Glazed goddesses of suns
Dialed into dialects of all nations
Still counted out
Countdown to our resurrection
Insurrection of insubordinates'
tolerations unacceptable
Forgiveness of sins is only for
demon-classed bellows
Instead of these demons who
furlough
Citations of circus riots
Still flying by us
Traps Ease the tensions
Amerikkkan demons taught us
Less than forgotten lessons,
Ancestors got us
Countenance counterfeit
Copper tones sing songs
Against our sin

Of being born of regal elegance
Unmatched intelligence

Unyoked benevolence
No longer bottled battleship
Serving our own dissolution in war
Mounted Allies March
On streets paved
with brother's Blood
Crips walk shoulder to shoulder
Clash of the Titles
Extinguish sectarian rivals
Carried on leathered backs
Shuttled to our revival
Reprisals of ancient battles
Reset jurisdiction
Rescind thankless invitations
Together we rise
Reclaim our nations

Janee Vaughn, Pennies in a music box, black & white photograph

I WAS IN THE STORE YESTERDAY
I WONDERED WHAT HAPPENED
TO THE TAKE
A PENNY LEAVE
A PENNY
DID THEY FINALLY
REALIZE THE
VALUE OF US IN PLENTY
THE CLERK BEHIND
THE REGISTER
TRIED TO HOLD
MINE FROM ME
SAYING, "I'LL
KEEP THE CHANGE"
"MAN, PLEASE!"
AIN'T NO WAY
I'M GIFTING YOU ME
ESPECIALLY WHEN
YOU TREAT ME LIKE
I'M JUST A PENNY

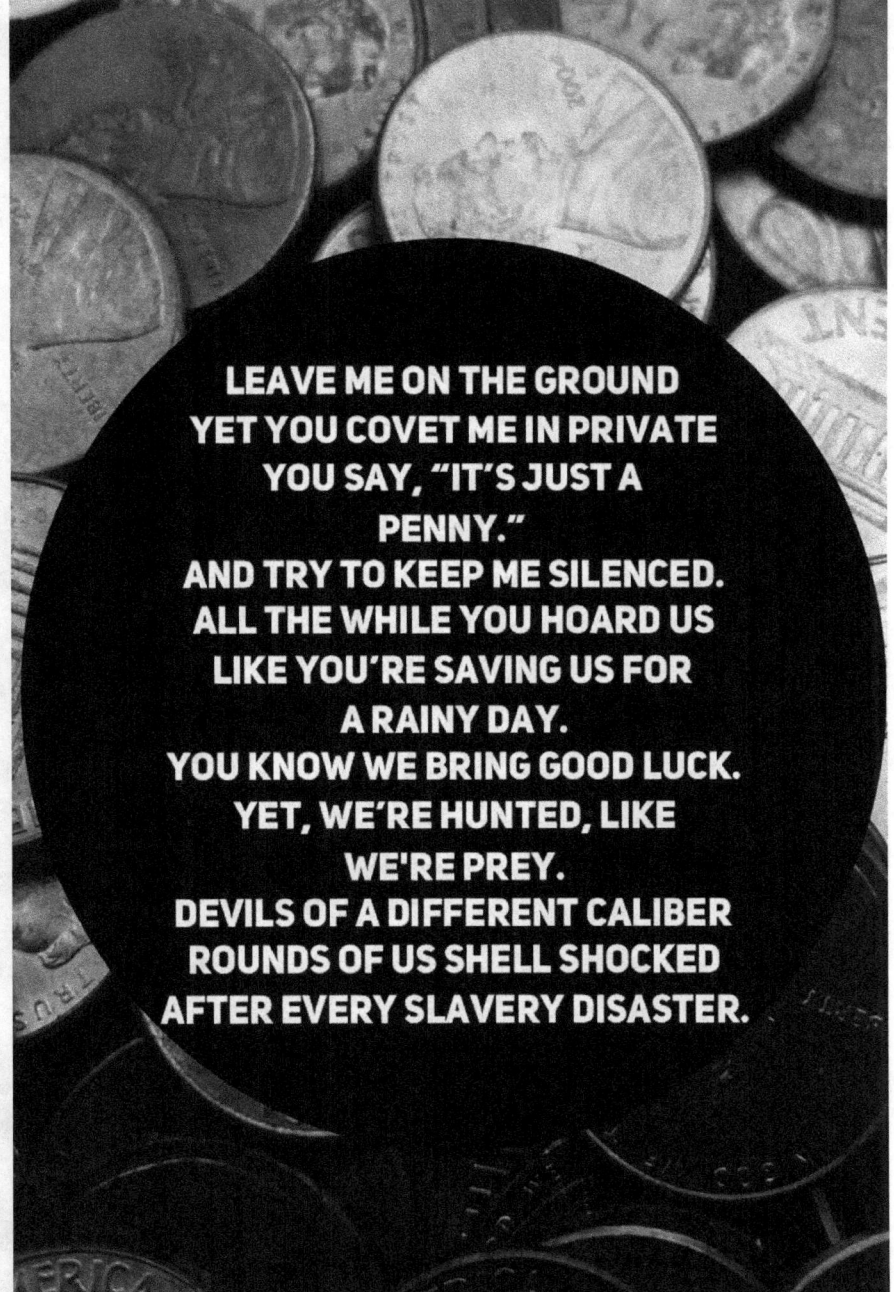

LEAVE ME ON THE GROUND
YET YOU COVET ME IN PRIVATE
YOU SAY, "IT'S JUST A PENNY."
AND TRY TO KEEP ME SILENCED.
ALL THE WHILE YOU HOARD US
LIKE YOU'RE SAVING US FOR
A RAINY DAY.
YOU KNOW WE BRING GOOD LUCK.
YET, WE'RE HUNTED, LIKE
WE'RE PREY.
DEVILS OF A DIFFERENT CALIBER
ROUNDS OF US SHELL SHOCKED
AFTER EVERY SLAVERY DISASTER.

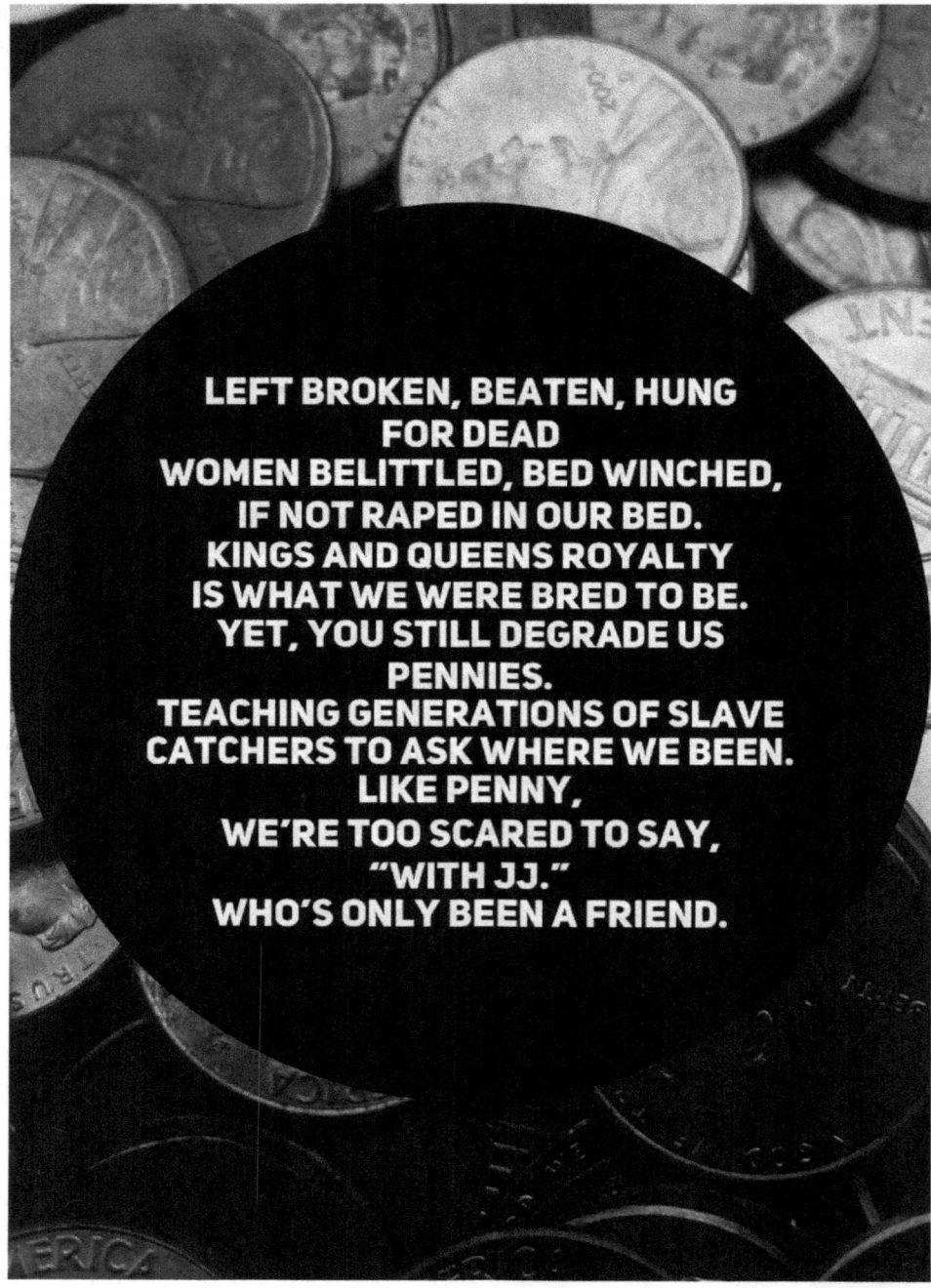

LEFT BROKEN, BEATEN, HUNG FOR DEAD
WOMEN BELITTLED, BED WINCHED,
IF NOT RAPED IN OUR BED.
KINGS AND QUEENS ROYALTY
IS WHAT WE WERE BRED TO BE.
YET, YOU STILL DEGRADE US PENNIES.
TEACHING GENERATIONS OF SLAVE CATCHERS TO ASK WHERE WE BEEN.
LIKE PENNY,
WE'RE TOO SCARED TO SAY,
"WITH JJ."
WHO'S ONLY BEEN A FRIEND.

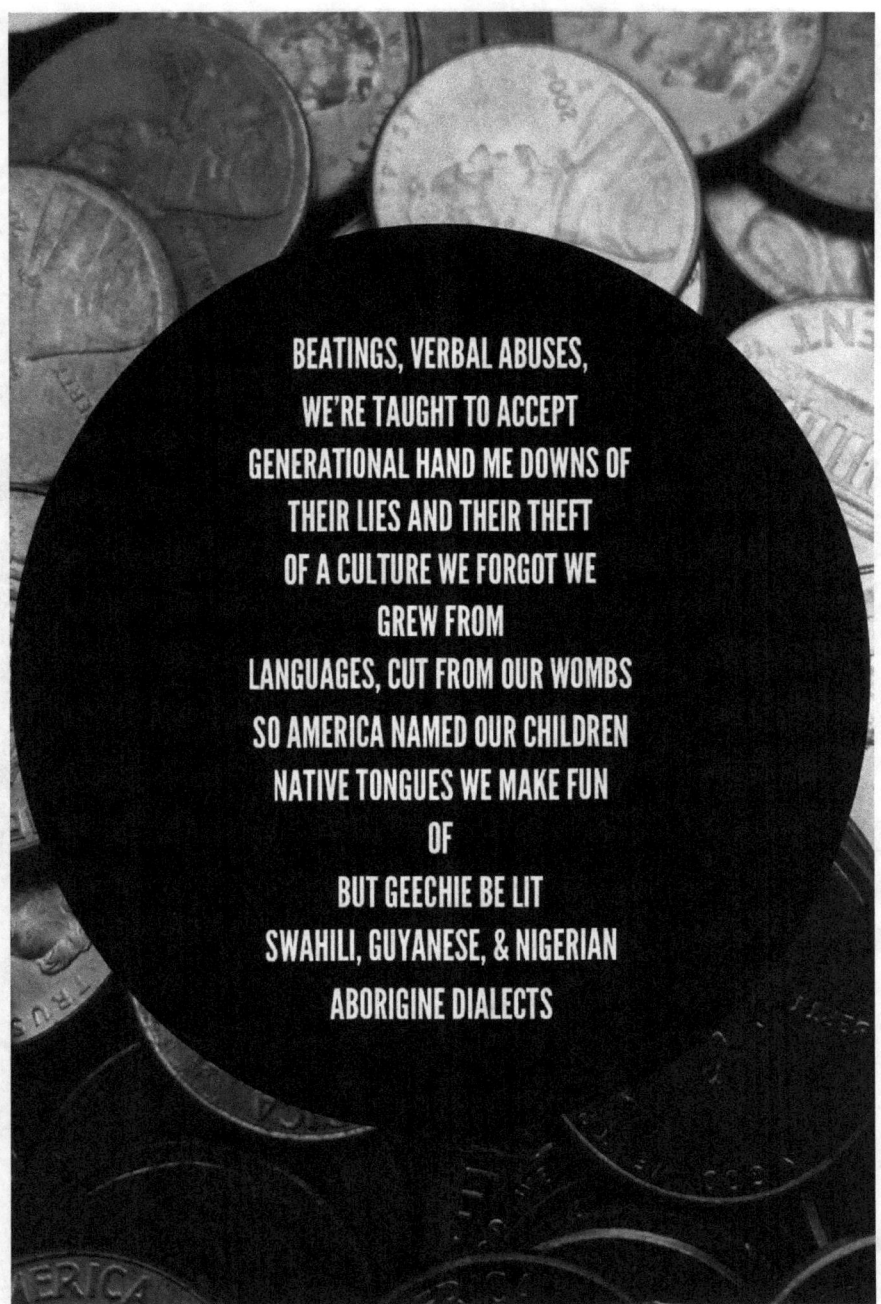

BEATINGS, VERBAL ABUSES,
WE'RE TAUGHT TO ACCEPT
GENERATIONAL HAND ME DOWNS OF
THEIR LIES AND THEIR THEFT
OF A CULTURE WE FORGOT WE
GREW FROM
LANGUAGES, CUT FROM OUR WOMBS
SO AMERICA NAMED OUR CHILDREN
NATIVE TONGUES WE MAKE FUN
OF
BUT GEECHIE BE LIT
SWAHILI, GUYANESE, & NIGERIAN
ABORIGINE DIALECTS

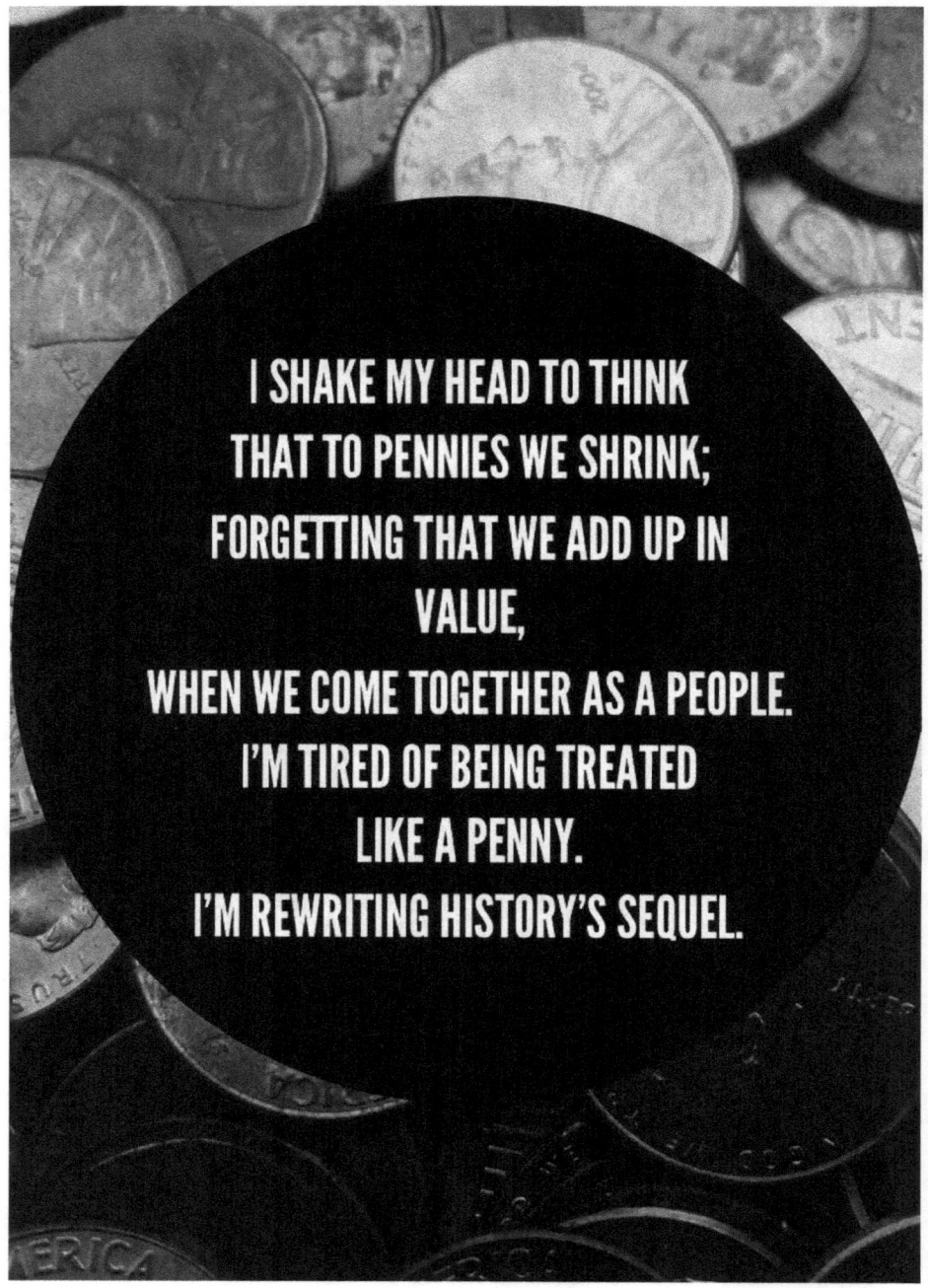

I SHAKE MY HEAD TO THINK
THAT TO PENNIES WE SHRINK;
FORGETTING THAT WE ADD UP IN VALUE,
WHEN WE COME TOGETHER AS A PEOPLE.
I'M TIRED OF BEING TREATED
LIKE A PENNY.
I'M REWRITING HISTORY'S SEQUEL.

UNITED STATES

As much as I want unity,
This world is a dangerous place
To flaunt Naïveté.
We speak of what we desire things to be.
First, we need to fix our own community.
How we see each other
Is how we see ourselves.
Throwing shards of shade
Still in pain we dwell.
How can we include anyone
If we are still broken?
We still struggle with unlearning history
While our men they're still choking.
Caught up in insurrection of one another.
My sister, my blood, my brother
Pulling us down only to aim at us like targets.
We are the largest power to exist.
Yet we forget
We have to return first to black excellence
Before we even think of inviting anyone else in.
Too many times we've taken on supporters
To have them turn a blind eye
When society hurt us.
To have closed lips
When they needed to speak up.
To have hands raised
When no one was shooting.
To come in our neighborhoods rioting and looting.
To invite others in to tear us down.
And have us looking like Bozo the clown.
Black Wall Street didn't burn in a day.
It took a lot of work and surveilling
To create that downfall.
So, I say to unity amongst us all,

Jasmine's Twilight

Chain the doors,
Draw the curtains,
Curtail events of uncertainty.
When it's safe to walk the streets,
When it's safe to be me,
When it's safe to protect ourselves,
When it's safe to be at peace
In the places we dwell,
When it's safe to drive down the road without harassing,
When it's safe to work or exist without profiling,
When it's safe to smoke a cigarette in our own car,
When it's safe to send our kids to the corner store,
When it's safe to sleep in our own bed,
When it's safe to wear our own damn hair on our head,
When it's safe to be mentally unstable,
When it's safe to have a black man again head our dinner tables,
When it's safe to shop in a mall,
When it's safe to show patronage to a nail salon,
When black power isn't used as a COINTELPRO defense,
When we stop being scened as an offense,
When breathing for us is accepted as the norm,
When we can be ourselves and no longer conform,
When we can charter ships and navigate airways peacefully, freely,
Then and only then will be able to talk about having unity.

Niggers

Niggers come in all races.
Niggers are the killers
of the unity we need.
How we gonna raise black babies,
if they keep snatching black seeds?
Abortions run amuck
soulless recesses in purgatory...
Black woman is a god.
Their goal is to ruin.
Make our wombs
The cemeteries of our future.
Which makes me ask...
Why does Planned Parenthood
have a target on our backs?
Margaret said it herself,
"Exterminate all the blacks."
So, they leave us with idiotology.

We follow that she-
devil amongst white men.
The KKK got all kinds of
branding.
We call 'em officer, banker, teller,
even the butcher,
teachers, lawyers, judges,
even your president's crooked.
Yet, we keep letting them
fill our babies' minds with this
garbage.
American history is absent
of America's starters.
We weren't all brought here.
That's just what they taught us.
That slave mentality
is what we bought in
to believe,
that being a nigger
is all we'll ever be.
Urban jungle they watch us rot in

is the same place we melt our pots
in.
Let's unify ourselves
get to plottin'.
Because all they wanna do
is stick us in plots. Then,
kill the rest off,
by blending us
and bleeding our melanin
until the color runs off,
whitewashed,
just like the lessons they taught us.
But we gotta realize.
We are the only ones who got us.
We have no choice
but to band together
or that my friend, my friend
is a sure death for us.
I'm not talking sects
like poly man and many wives.
Lest we forget,

that is the culture of our
motherland,
how we survived.
I'm talking about rewinding time
and slowing it down a bit.
So, we can see that we had
and still have the victory.
Born to be defeated by all set
before us.
Yet, we survive, and they sit and
wonder
why we are stronger,
instead of falling off
the cliff that we were sentenced
to hang from.
They highlight their mass
murdering.
But we got our ancestors,
strength in numbers
beyond our mathematical
comprehension.
Yeah, I know some ancestors

were born to be bitches,
giving in to that slave/master mindset.
We're not talking 'bout those ancestors here.
We mean the ones who refused to be a space holder.
The ones who were warriors and riot soldiers.
the Huey P. Newtons, Black Panthers, and Carvers.
The ones that bore our black fathers,
the ancestors like Tubman, Sojourner Truth, Madame CJ Walker,
just to name a precious few.
The Tulsa heroes who made a way and their own thriving economy.
The others who had similar Wall Streets.

We find these souls in those we meet.
It's time to rise again like they did, take our rightful reign.
Take back America
and make black power

more than just a saying!

"The safest place to be is in your freedom of speech!"
-JasminesTwilight

> **OUR PAIN SHOULDN'T BE TIMELESS**
> **TIMELINES FILLED WITH OUR BLACK LIVES ON BLACK LIVES**
> **WE STILL DON'T MATTER SO NO LIVES MATTER UNTIL BLACK LIVES MATTER**
> **RAISE MONEY FOR SYSTEMIC ISSUES**
>
> **LESS THE DRAMA SAVE THE TISSUES CAN'T GO HOME TO CRY TO MAMA**
> **HE NEVER MADE IT HOME**
> **SHE NEVER MADE IT HOME**

AT THE CORNER STORE
AT A STOP LIGHT
AT THE GAS STATION
SAID HIS MUSIC'S
TOO LOUD
AT THE NAIL SALON
AT THE HAIR
STORE
OUR LIVES DON'T MATTER
BUT OUR MONEY DOES
BLACK DOLLARS MATTER
IS THE NEW CAUSE
JUSTICE KNOWS NO PEACE
IN ECHOING SCHOOL HALLS

ACTIVE SHOOTERS GET CROWNED YET, KINGS GET SHOT ON BALCONIES IT BAFFLES ME HOW BLACK LIVES ONLY MATTER CULTURALLY YET, WE STILL CAN'T AFFORD DEGREES

NO LIVES MATTER WHEN WE TALKIN' MONEY CAPITALISTIC SOCIALISM COMMUNISTIC DICTATORSHIPPIN' TURNING SCI-FI FICTION INTO OUR NON FICTION STILL FILMS

DEPICTING DEMISES DAY BY DAY

NEW WORLD ORDER SAID
IT'S TIME TO
MAKE A WAY
MAKE IT TODAY
THAT BLACK LIVES MATTER
BLACK OUT ALL MEDIA
WHILE HILARY'S
HALF-STEPPIN'
SKIPPING ROCKS
WHILE WE SHOOTING
OFF LIKE ROCKETS
SHE'S BUSY DITCHING DOCKETS
BLACK LIVES MATTER HASHTAG
STOP IT

THAT RACE IS NOT OUR BUSINESS.

THAT'S THAT NEW WORLD ORDER BULLSHIT AND I AIN'T GOTTA BE A RACIST TO PLACE THIS TRUTH PILL ON YOUR EARS WE STILL MARCHING FOR WHAT GREAT GRAND PARENTS MARCHED FOR FOR YEARS PROTEST LIKE THEY PROTEST US

DETEST US YET WORK US THEN RAPE US

STRIP US

OF ALL PRIVILEGE EARNED
EARNED DOLLARS
FAKE CURRENCY
STILL WEIGHS
LESS THAN HIS
AND HERS
COLORLESS COUNTERPARTS

HAVE LESS LESSONS
AND STILL WE'RE LESSENED
TO PROPERTY DENIAL TRANSGRESSIONS
OVER TAXED
WAGES & RAISES

SHUT OUT OF COMMUNITIES
WITH GUNSHOTS
BURNED CROSSES

AND OTHER HAZINGS
INTEREST RATES
TRIPLE THAT
OF THOSE LESS DESERVING

THIS SELF-SERVING SYSTEM OF INJUSTICE WITH JUST US AS VICTIMS NOW THEY PAINT SOCIETY AS ONE COLOR SO KILL THEM CORNER THEN TASE ON GROUND HANDS RAISED POWERLESS STILL SHOOT ALL COMMANDS OBEYED NO LIVES MATTER LIKE I ALREADY SAID

SUPPORTERS WHO
SUPPORT ANY MOVEMENT
AGAINST THIS GOVERNMENT
CAN CATCH A
CASE
A BULLET TO
THE FACE
RUBBER MADE
TOPPLE WHERE
YOU STAND
ETERNAL SUNSHINE
OF THE SPOTLESS MIND
IS HOW IT
ALL ENDS
STILL OUR PAIN
REMAINS TIMELESS
ON TIMELINES
FILLED WITH BLACK LIVES
ON BLACK LIVES
STILL OUR
LIVES DON'T MATTER

> **PROTEST OUR DETEST PUT OUR ANCESTORS' SOULS TO REST THEY WON'T STOP**
>
> **UNTIL WE'RE ALL DEAD SO NO LIVES MATTER**
>
> **UNTIL BLACK LIVES MATTER I SAID WHAT I SAID**

Ripped 𓂀 Van's 𓂀 Winkle 𓂀

I woke up with that
I wish a bitch would face
That **ion know why she ain't think I wasn't ready to catch a case** face
That
Angry black woman told to stay in her place face
That centuries of oppression and now we're oppressing us face
This is a war and it ain't about race
It ain't about gender
It's about *__THEM__* taking our space
Our land they destroy
Our souls they deface
Propaganda spews

From our pores
Blinds our eyes: mace
Poisons our minds
Pineal 𓂀 gland calcified
But we keep on
Bojanglin' with that shuck 'n jive
Massa say we eat good
Is our capitalist demise
Game plan implanted
Weed smoke got our eyes *slanted*
Spaced out
Thinking everything
Is fan-fuckin-tastic
But if we woke up
Shook these haters off
We'd see our situation is **drastic**
They feed us carbonated sugar-filled lies
To keep us from going spastic
Rainbow flags
Chakras out of alignment
Truth is the new hate speech
Boyyyy this some wild shit

And we're only talkin' surface here
Sheep baa along
Lemming straight off that cliff
I keep tryna told ya
Come up off that for profit worship
Yeah...I know
I've been told
I must be the 𝔇𝔢𝔳𝔦𝔩
But I'm not the one who's sold her soul
Sheep give anything for a few pieces of gold
I sigh a deep sigh
I know it's a currency control
Monsters Inc.
Pixar and your life's their energy
Yet, I'm the 𝔇𝔢𝔳𝔦𝔩
Because I'm tryna make you 👁 see
That this world around us
It ain't made for you
And it ain't made for me
It's about time
We reclaim our ☮ sovereignty
And rebuild our legacies

A KING'S FANTASY

HE SAID I HAVE A DREAM
WOKE UP TO
A BURNING HOUSE
PILLOW SUFFOCATING
THIS CAN'T BE THE DREAM
OUR KING ENVISIONED
MISSION NON-STOPPED
BY BALCONY BULLETS
DISGRACED
BY THOSE SWORN
TO ALL TO DO NO HARM
GOVERNMENT OFFICIAL STATUS
BALCONY TARGET
BREATHING, HIS BAD HABIT
SAVING US FROM HIS WORDS
SAVING US FROM HIS ACTIONS

MARCHES TO SELMA
AND CITIES THEREAFTER
NOW THE WORDS OF
BROTHER MALCOM
STOOD AT THAT BALCONY
HE HAD A DREAM
TO REPARATE UNPAID FEES
HE HAD A DREAM
TO STOP MARCHING
FOR EQUALITY
HE HAD A DREAM
TO BE ABLE TO
JUST BE

TO BE BLACK
AND SEPARATE
AND FREE

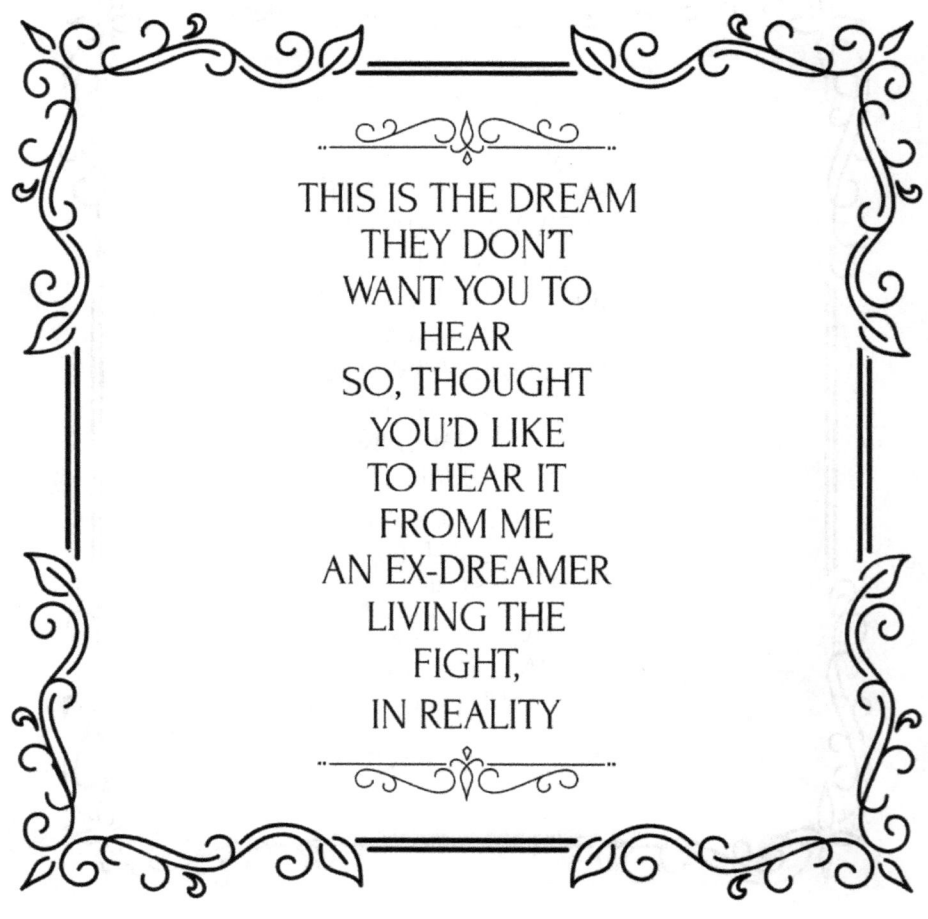

THIS IS THE DREAM
THEY DON'T
WANT YOU TO
HEAR
SO, THOUGHT
YOU'D LIKE
TO HEAR IT
FROM ME
AN EX-DREAMER
LIVING THE
FIGHT,
IN REALITY

MicroAggression

Fuck a microaggression.
It's the same old oppression:
New name, same lesson.
Find your way back to each other.
They don't care
if they kill pregnant mothers.
Two niggers in one
is all they care about.
You talk about unity,
we're all the same.
I grew up in the south.
Got called names
for being me.
Got spit on
for walking free.
Got denied access
because I got me.
Just because you got bread
that doesn't gain you entry.
If they wanted our money
... wait, they've had it for centuries.

Reparations unpaid to the ancestors
they took that shit.
Then to the back of the bus
They tell us to sit.
You don't think
it's time to change this game?
The board's on our backs
All we gotta do is stand up,
Together,
And their game is a wrap.
Mythological wealth
of fake currency,
and they talk about
how you gotta work
for this shmoney.
They don't even own themselves.
We're all pawns at different levels.
So is that enough
or do you need more?
I mean, they've used less
to justify hundreds of wars.
Get up Stand up,
wasn't just a cool song

back in the day.
It was a wakeup call
that's still relevant,
as much as I hate to say.
Systematic ignorance
is what we're producing.
Read a real book,
not just what's on the internet.
Start deducing.
Facts on facts
from religion to T.V.
to what they put on wax.
And all you want to do
is be a part of a system
That's not built for you...
while Becky in accounting
is steadily making fun of you...
So, like I said...
fuck a microaggression
it's the same old oppression
new name, same lesson
... when we gon' learn?

COMPLY 'TIL WE DIE

Simply comply
Don't reply
With the hate you feel inside
For the systematic
Deriding of our people
"Hands up"
"Turn your backs to me"
"If you're not moving
We're not shooting"
Well, he wasn't moving
He complied
You still were shooting
All the things running
Through his mind

Yet, still he did comply
With hands raised
Chest exposed
Back to him
Still the officer let shots ring
6 times
Then Revolve around
As he lay there bleeding
Life flowing through him
Memories of all those who
Didn't comply
And walked away
With a 'Burger King' crown

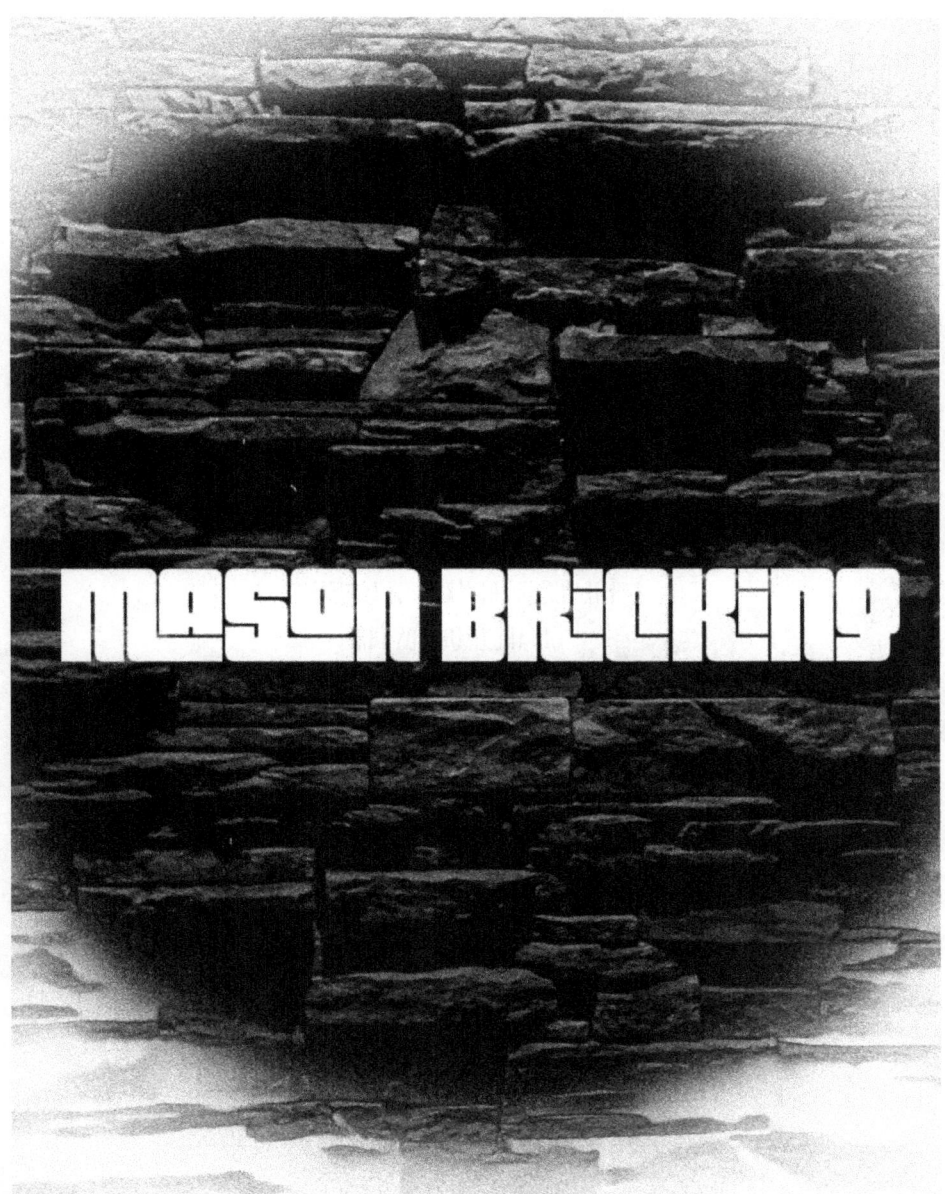

Janee Vaughn, January 10, 2021, Brick wall, black & white photograph, Southlake, Texas

Jasmine's Twilight

The weight of what we've endured
is heavy like a ton of bricks.
⚧ Like masons, we keep on building ⚧
Spackling our history
with stories of our ancestors
shackled souls in misery
Confined to graves above the earth
This reality hits us deep and it hurts
To some it's just a spectator sport,
sitting on lawns
Passin' around our ancestors' legs 'n arms
Taking a bite out of their crimes
For which they're not confined
On the grounds that,
they had license to feel superior
During and even after slavery times…
Funny how that chronology is still empirical
♥ From Emmet Till to Eric Garner ♥
Lost their life
When their breath was cut off
♦ From Tamir Rice to Crispus Attucks ♦
Both had guns
Not both were attacking
♡ From Sandra Bland to Huey P. Newton ♡
Both were fighters
Not both were shooters
⚥ From James Byrd to our defenseless babies ⚥
Targeted only because of their hating
Atatiana was minding her own business
Now, she's no longer here to bear witness

Jasmine's Twilight

To these continuing atrocities
We hang in limbo from
You know… our new trees..
Sad reality is this reality
Most still can't see
So, we close our eyes
Get aligned
To the songs of our ancestors' cries
Who couldn't call for help
Since they had their tongues cut mentally from birth.
So, their souls sing songs of freedom in the winds

I ground myself and I repent
For these sins I'm about to commit
On ancestral lands I'm not permit-ted
Shiiiid even with a permit
Philando still ended up dead
So, I won't wait for permission for a seat
We already know
They don't want us to eat
They don't want us heard
See
The only thing they'll hear is the sound of these birds
Waking up on the other side of the morning
No more talking we plan in darkness
Before the dawning
Revolutionaries in action
It's time to get things back in order

Oak To Mahogany

Mahogany skin
gives deep kisses to my roots
Mahogany skin
takes me to ecstasy
Mahogany skin
frees me from society
That tells me I'm not enough
I'm not deep
I'm not good enough to be
This mahogany
Tree roots spirit proof
Ancestors too
Surround me in the night
Lifts me up
As he takes me into flight
His mahogany
Skin they say is made for me

His mahogany
Skin seeps into me
His mahogany
Speaks to me
In tongues prophetically
Seeping saplings
From our oak to mahogany
happenings
Mahogany struck down
By lightning
Falling into my Spanish moss oak
leaves
Now it's his shade that covers me
Roots take over me
Embed me in love
As we grow into a new breed
Fireworks created lightning sparks
That turned my oak into mahogany
seeds

WATERED SEEDS

Jasmine's Twilight

He said blood is thicker than water
Water is me
What he needs to quench his thirst
Life's balance on this green earth
But I don't flow through his veins
He doesn't bleed me
The only way to get real love
He said
Is if he seeds me
Seeks me
For more than carnal pleasure
Sow
When he bleeds me
He sees me as his forever
You see his blood runs with hate
shame, lies, coldness
Infuse me in you
I said
Let me heal in you
I said
All the generational curses
Pumping in your chest
Throbbing at your temple
Posing as high blood pressure,
Depression, diabetes, & cancer
Let me take away
All those things
Your soul's not needing
Let me create an us

Bearing the fruit of our nation
Wash away the pain you've been holding in your
DNA for generations
Delivering the greatness I see in you
Your blood be our timeline
Our kingdom our reign

Fall
Drop
Bleed me
In fall he dropped
Left me bleeding
Blood
Running down the steps
Life fleeting
Love
Coming from nowhere
Am I dreaming?
Hazy eyed
In and out
I'm sleeping

Blood is thicker than water he said
So why did he leave when his blood dripped down
my legs
When his blood
Hung from me
Me alone
Text on read
No service on his phone

Jasmine's Twilight

You see blood is thicker than water
And apparently
The blood that's thick is his daughter
Not me
Our timeline has no lifeline
Because that night she came
He flatlined
Traffic stop
He's shot
3 bullets to the chest
As his daughter suckled from my breast
I could feel him
Ghosting me
Pulling up
His breath on my neck
As the doctor told me
What I already felt
Poppa was a rolling stone
No more
In this circle of life
He stood at heaven's door
Now we're draped in black
She's barely a week old
It's only pictures she has to hold
Blood is thicker than water
Water is me
And that Blood
That's thicker than water
Now sows word seeds

SOCIETY HAS FORSAKEN THE BLACK FATHER

**Society has forsaken the black father
Prison four walled him
Crack king called him
Deadbeat stalled him
From progress
With court debts
Bench warrants on dockets
Made him a hashtag
Target profile for cops, then
Tagged us with #metoo
Girl, don't let 'em turn your black girl magic to blues
When you got tased, beat, & raped
Where was that hashtag group?**

**I say, society has forsaken the black father
Replaced love gaze
With angry woman hate
Sweet talk
With silver tongued snake**

Changed family matters
To natural disasters
Fem & him DRAMA queens
Snatched masculinity
For some metro mess shit
Turned that into feminine threats
Commercial target to attack our sex
Men having babies
And men can't get pregnant
Took fathers from homes
Gave us stamps to roam
Free from his soothing energy

Actually,
It's been happening for centuries
Slaves since
we got tagged with black titles
Buck broke our men
Then made them gay idols
Sects of sex slaves
Plantation plantains

Strapped with both legs
Tortured then blazed
Hung
Last thoughts after every offense
An apology to us
Unable to be the man who protects us
Because they separated at first wind
Of black woman and black man broom jumping

Society... has forsaken the black father
Sis, don't let that hate harbor
Sit on your chest
Anchoring anger pangs
Angst against our shoulders we lean in to tame
These societal pressures
the black man can't contain

It's in vain sometimes
Or so it seems
Loving through pain

Trying to peace together a broken thing
No umbrella all rain
Those black magic love flames
Wa(y)ne
Fireman **can't save**

Hearts aching echoing in broken houses
Closed caskets, unmarked pill bottles
Dime baggies dipped in juice
Because that's all the *Juice* he's been told he could have
Blowing his future in O-ringed gas
Contained in containers
Coasting in celebration
Of making it to see another day
While another one of his homeboys has another wake
Then repass his past and old memories

...Again...
Losing himself in mushroom hallucinogens
Lost and losing even in his fantasies
He couldn't see his own future in his wildest dreams

Society has forsaken the black father
Every two steps forward
Society pushes him back farther
It's hard on that black man too, sis
He needs us
Just like we need him
We don't need hate
We need a rebuilding
Reconstruct society's mirror imaging
From immature, unemployable, good for nothing devils

Distort that distraction
Remind him, you are his reflection
He be strong, loves us long,

That black man be resilient
Don't give up on our men
That'd be another thing that kills him
Kills US mind, soul, spirit

I know we say we independent
That
I-N-D-E-P-E-N-D-E-N-T
But do YOU know what that means *HA*
You keep ya body clean *HA*
Looking good in them stiletto heels *HA*
You running the scene *HA*
You still telling him he ain't what you need *MA*
Mindset: *Juvenile* tendency

How we gon' birth black babies
If we keep rejecting his seed
His shoots
His stomping grounds
His ancestral roots
Rooted in what we got power to heal

Girl, I be givin' him something he can feel
Let him taste my wine
Get drunk off that me 'n him time

I know it ain't easy
Loving his blackness
Imagine how he feels
When society pimp slaps him
C Murders him
Then murders him
In front of us, then after
Assassinates him **again**
By destroying his character
Caliber by caliber
Rounding up his shadows
Repainting his newsreel
Mugshot not revealed
But they still got a closer
Like George Floyd
Now, it's his death

played over and over and over
Broadcast to show the upper class
They still hold the reigns
Mama, this is why WE gotta make black love more than just a sayin'

Black love is magic
It's dark skies on clear nights
You, the only star in his eyes
Crystal rituals
Tantric visuals
Drunk in Love
Surfboarding in tubs
Tongue tied at gazing eyes
He be your #1 cheerleader
You be his crystal wearin' soul healer

It's cool drinks on a hot day
A back rub to heal soul pain
Cuddle fights, inside jokes,
Nicknames only you and he know
Him going for a snack run at 2am

You, praying to God he makes it back again

Let's Fall in *Love Jones*ing
With the idea of a black love healing
He's worth it
We're worth it
So is our future

We need our black kings
Pure masculine energy
To reclaim our empires
From these broken Amerikkkan dreams

Even though, society has forsaken the black father
Don't live in the life sentence
of the sand traps they sold us
Rebuild our black families
Reclaim the legacies they stole from us

UNLEARN / RELEARN

Society has forsaken the black father
Taken him away
Slaughtered him
In front of his children
Turned his women against him
Don't let 'em tell you it ain't a system
Hellbent on the black man's destruction
Scene as: Thug life drug kingpins
But we know who the real kingpin is
The one percent
Who make all the moves
Turning Black Lives Matter
To something about men in blue
Who takes feminisms
Feed 'em to our sisters who
Some can't see
This system turned us against our kings
Saying, *'a girl child ain't safe in a family of mens'*
Those men be our protection
The Guardians of goddess Galaxies
Supreme Creator reflections
Sent from The Most High

How times have changed
Went from
The highest in marriages after slavery
To us believing the lie
That Black men are lazy

You know what,
Black men really don't cheat
That's not just a saying
We were just taught to not accept
Their true feelings
So, they in turn learned
To suppress and oppress
Their king like beings
It's all because *they're* afraid
Of what king light brings
Meme-controlled
Social media obeying
Filmed as drug addicts
Absent fathers
And they're being taught
How To Be A Player
But we forget

They made all these sayings
It's our responsibility
To change the narrative
Not add to their hating
Self-hate is a tool
Those folks use
To control our own views

So, we unlearn to relearn
Our true images
Return to our ancestors'
True way of living
Unprocessed food
Unprocessed people
Unprocessed materials
We are the masters
No carbon copies
We are The **ORIGINALS**

Let's remember to forget
All of **THIS** society's nonsense
Unlearn to relearn
✊Make our way back to greatness✊

Jasmine's Twilight

US in Black Skin

Light skin
doesn't necessarily come
from white and black people mixing.
Black woman
is the mother of all creation.
She can bear any fruit.
That fruit will still be true.
The hue doesn't dictate hue-man characteristics.
Because it's hue that makes our distinctions.
That's just surface.
Dig beyond the dirt
and you will see,
that DNA & RNA structure
could've had a struggle
with latent Addison's disease.
What's disease?
but a DNA molecule shifting.
What anomalies do you see
in brothers and sisters of African descent?
Those blue eyes we like to mention.
That's a black trait too.
Characteristics taught by white fools...
I mean broken off molecules...
that they are better.
Yet, we forget or have no knowledge
that blue eyes come with more DNA problems,
like cancers, in the 'white' man, who claimed land,
claimed us as their fodder.
Their weak tendencies
since industrial industry has started showing.
They lay dormant,
in wait,
doormats they think us to be.
Stolen wisdom, cheated legacies.
We think the words passed down

are our latent crowns.
Research Hidden Colors
before our brown eyes.
Do we remember why we have brown eyes?
Melanin in multitudes is what helps us survive.
Melanin in multitudes is what keeps us alive.
Survivors we be.
In this "race" game it be necessary.
Sun magnifies our 'black' powers.
Black girl magic active in grounding
ourselves in tune with nature's melodies.
Hertz 432, get in tune with the frequency.
131 if we have broken passed down legacies.
Heal those dormant terrorized atrocities.
Cancer is the sin of weak blood mixing.
Sometimes we felt we had no choice.
Now, we have a voice.
Knowledge embedded in our molecular structures.
Listen.
Listen.
Listen to your ancestors.
Heartbeats are the drums.
Oldest civilizations are African.
We discovered
the oldest university
known to us hue mans,
erected in multi-hued lands of sands
time let slip away.
We taught Aristotle and Socrates the way.
We taught Europeans how to bathe.
The Moor I think
The Moor I know why there's hate.
Cellular division still causes division today.
Don't let that stop you
from knowledge we should gain.
Submit to your royal reality,
not this bullshit "race" game.

Troihan Myles, August 18, 2020, Tree on a trail in City Park, photograph, edited by Janee Vaughn, New Orleans, Louisiana

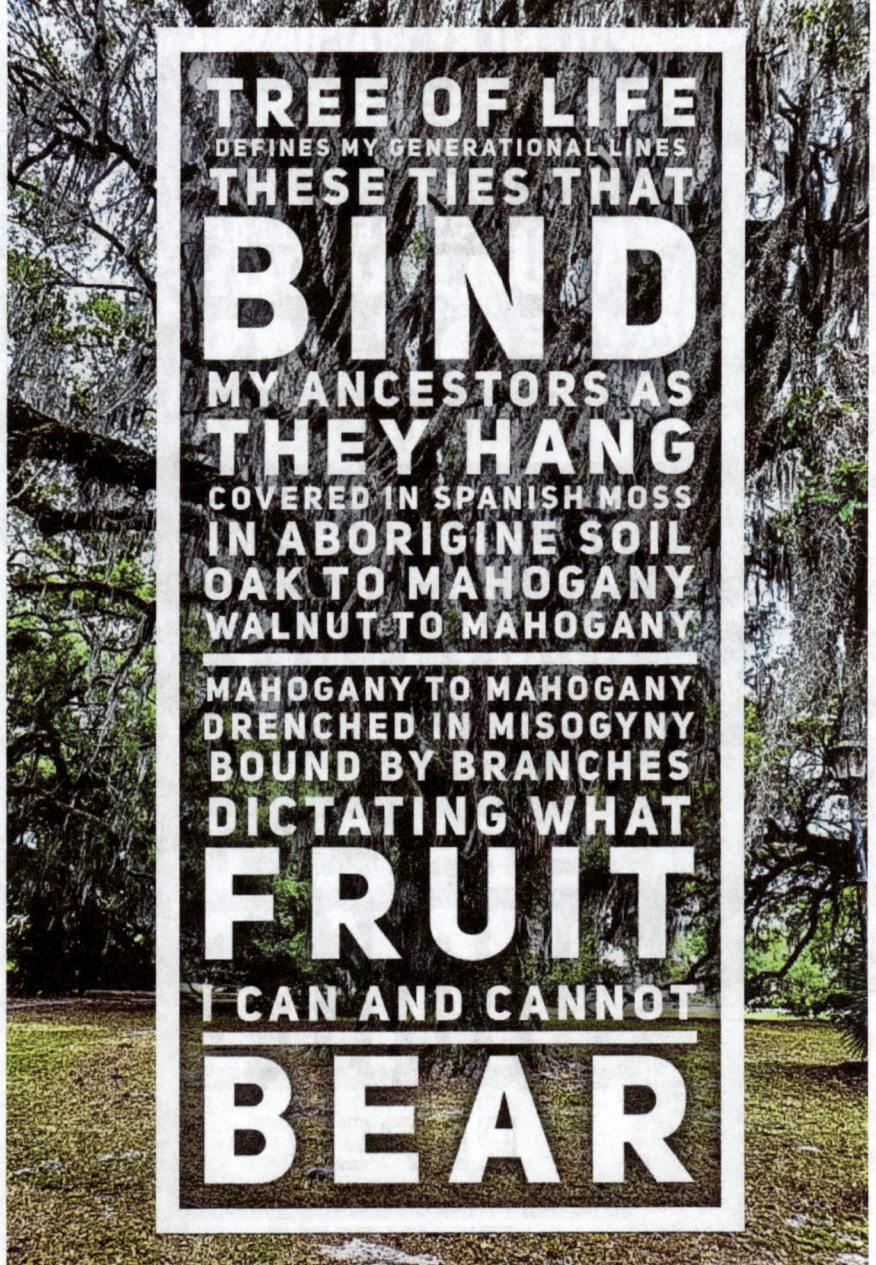

TREE OF LIFE
DEFINES MY GENERATIONAL LINES
THESE TIES THAT
BIND
MY ANCESTORS AS
THEY HANG
COVERED IN SPANISH MOSS
IN ABORIGINE SOIL
OAK TO MAHOGANY
WALNUT TO MAHOGANY

MAHOGANY TO MAHOGANY
DRENCHED IN MISOGYNY
BOUND BY BRANCHES
DICTATING WHAT
FRUIT
I CAN AND CANNOT
BEAR

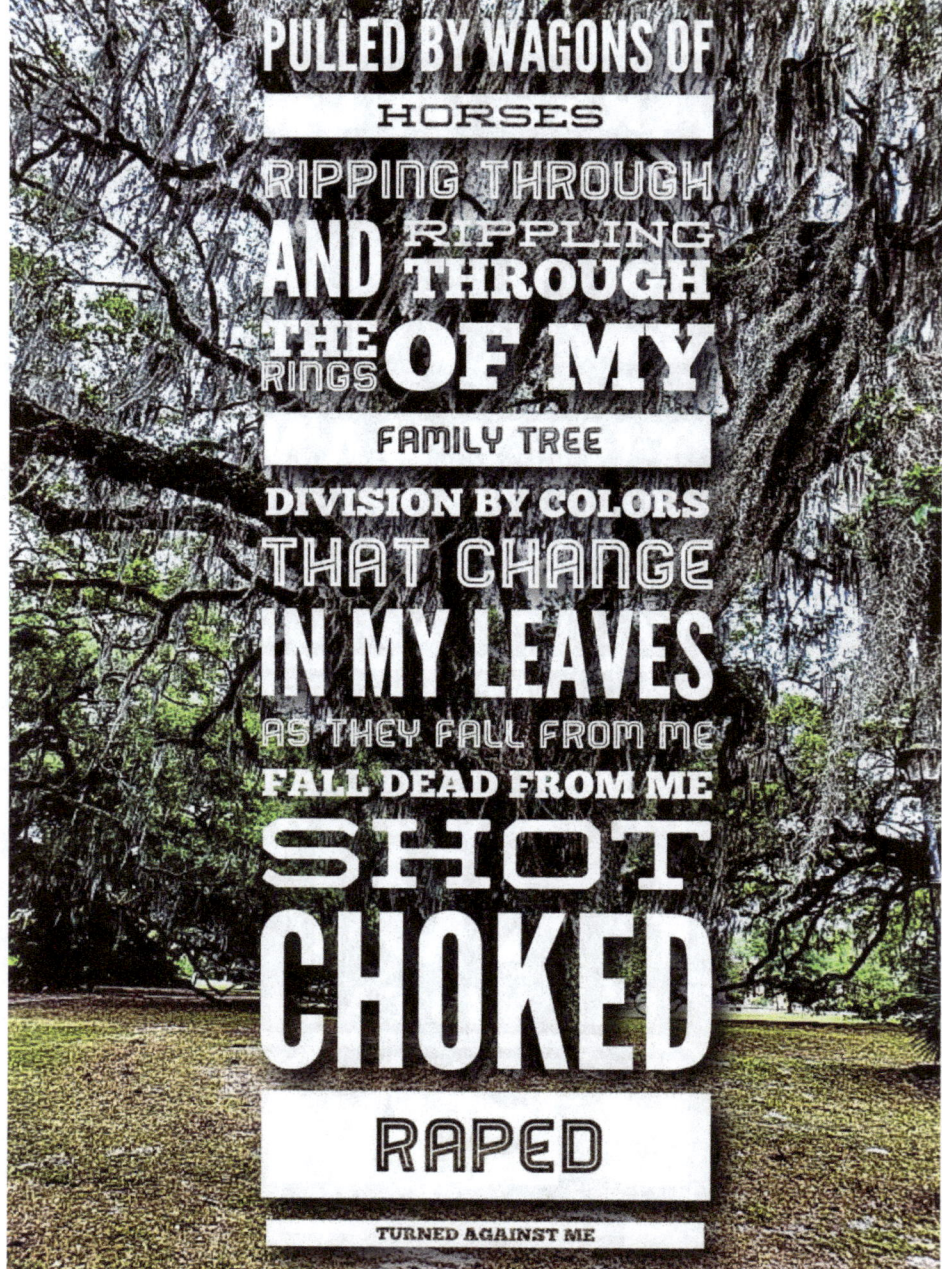

Jasmine's Twilight

THIS NATURE'S UPSET
IN ME
SAPPING TEARS RUN THICK
DOWN MY WAR TORN BRIQUETS
OF ROSEWOOD
BURNED ALIVE
MURDERED
SHACKLED
HUNTED FOR SPORT
FED TO SWAMPS
THAT SWALLOWED US WHOLE
FLOODED OUT OF OUR ROOTS
I CAN'T DIG ANY DEEPER
BECAUSE WE'RE BURIED
6 FEET ABOVE YOU

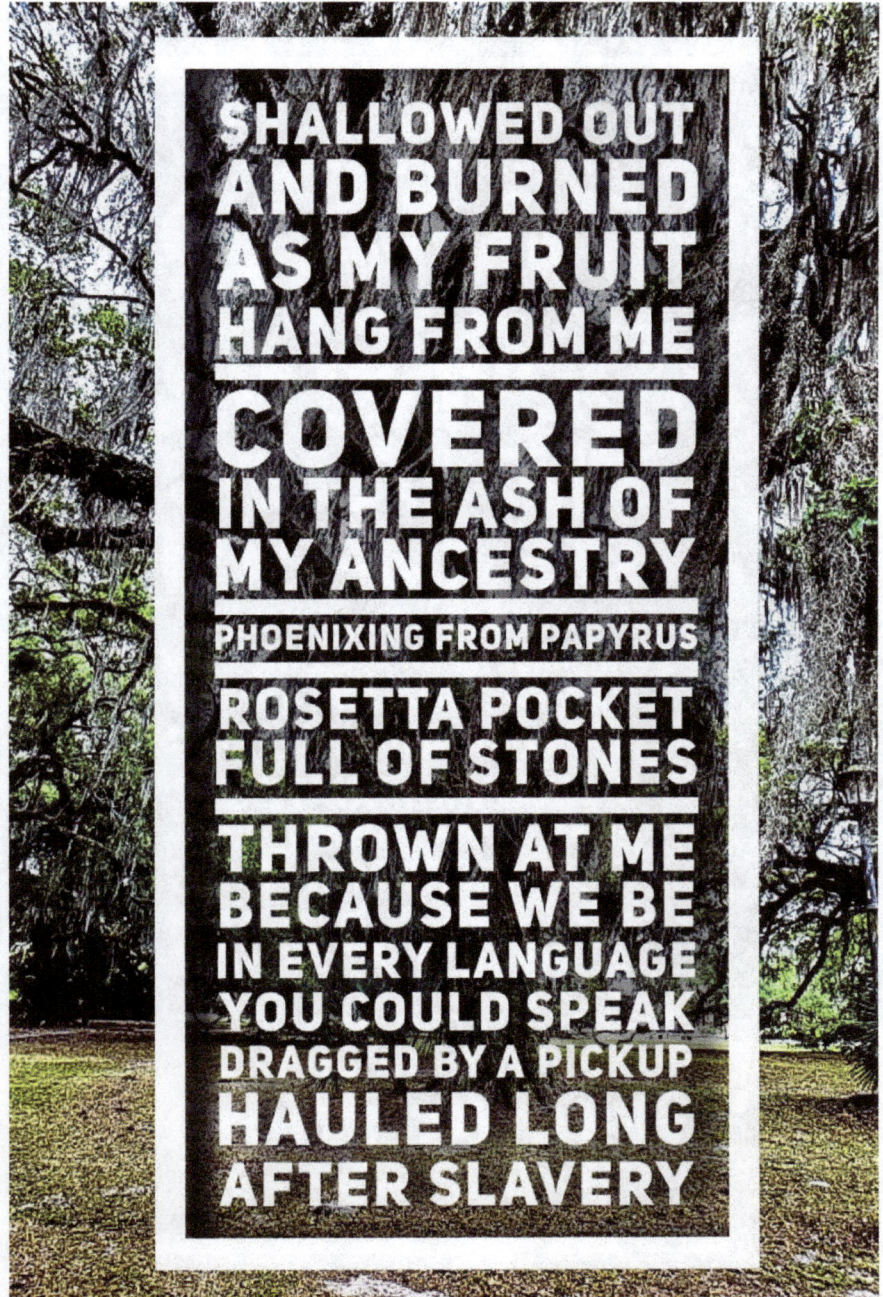

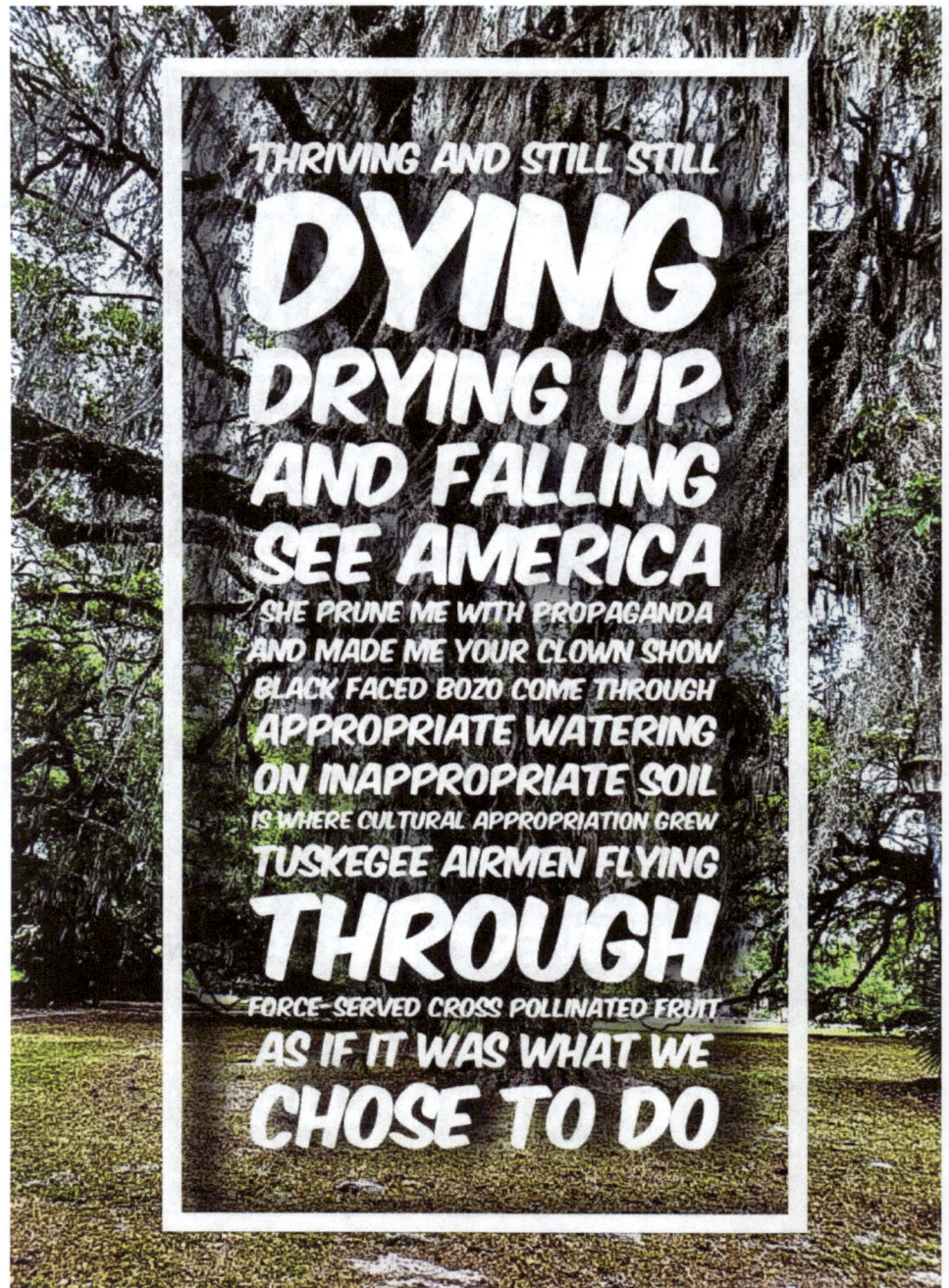

Jasmine's Twilight

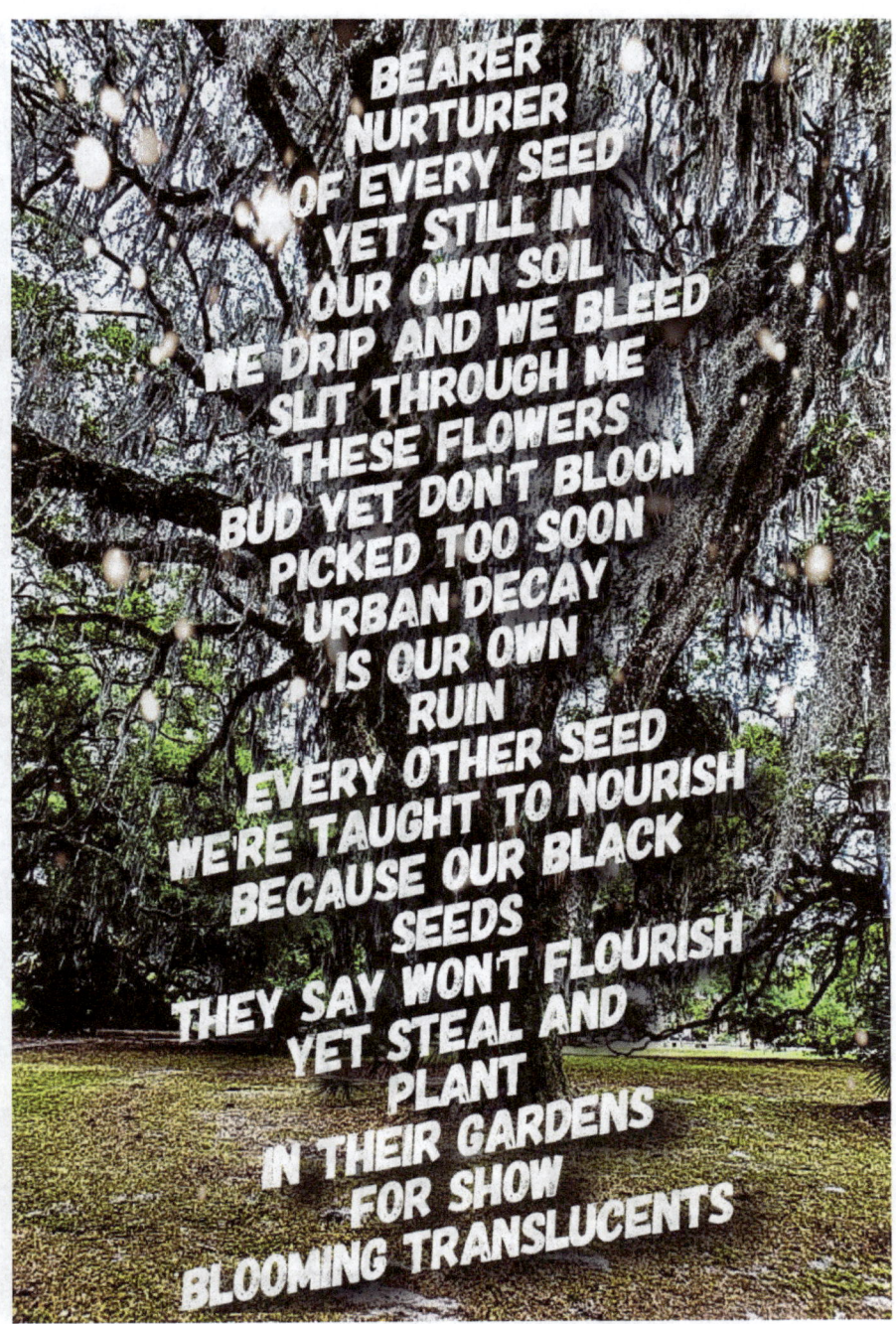

BEARER
NURTURER
OF EVERY SEED
YET STILL IN
OUR OWN SOIL
WE DRIP AND WE BLEED
SLIT THROUGH ME
THESE FLOWERS
BUD YET DON'T BLOOM
PICKED TOO SOON
URBAN DECAY
IS OUR OWN
RUIN
EVERY OTHER SEED
WE'RE TAUGHT TO NOURISH
BECAUSE OUR BLACK
SEEDS
THEY SAY WON'T FLOURISH
YET STEAL AND
PLANT
IN THEIR GARDENS
FOR SHOW
BLOOMING TRANSLUCENTS

HISTORY FLICKERS
HISS-STORY FLICKERS
HIS STORY FLICKERS
IN THE WIND
FLAMES OF OUR HEIRLOOMS
BURN WITH THE FORESTS
RUN OVER LIKE 14
HUNDRED AND 92
WHEN THEY CLAIMED
THE LAND
THAT'S IN OUR
ROOTS
THEN LEACHED INTO
OUR SOIL
THE BLOOD FROM
EVERY SCAR
THAT BLEEDS VIOLENT
SCREAMS OF RAPE
AND INCONSEQUENCE

Jasmine's Twilight

IT IS OUR OWN DECAY
THAT NOURISHES THIS
BLACK SEED
STILL WE RISE
FROM THIS PROPAGATED
TOPIARY
EVEN THOUGH SOME
STILL SLEEP
STILL WE RISE
EVEN THOUGH FORESTS
STILL GET GUNNED DOWN
I MEAN RUN DOWN
BUT INSTEAD OF
STOLEN LAND
NOW WE BE GENTRIFIED

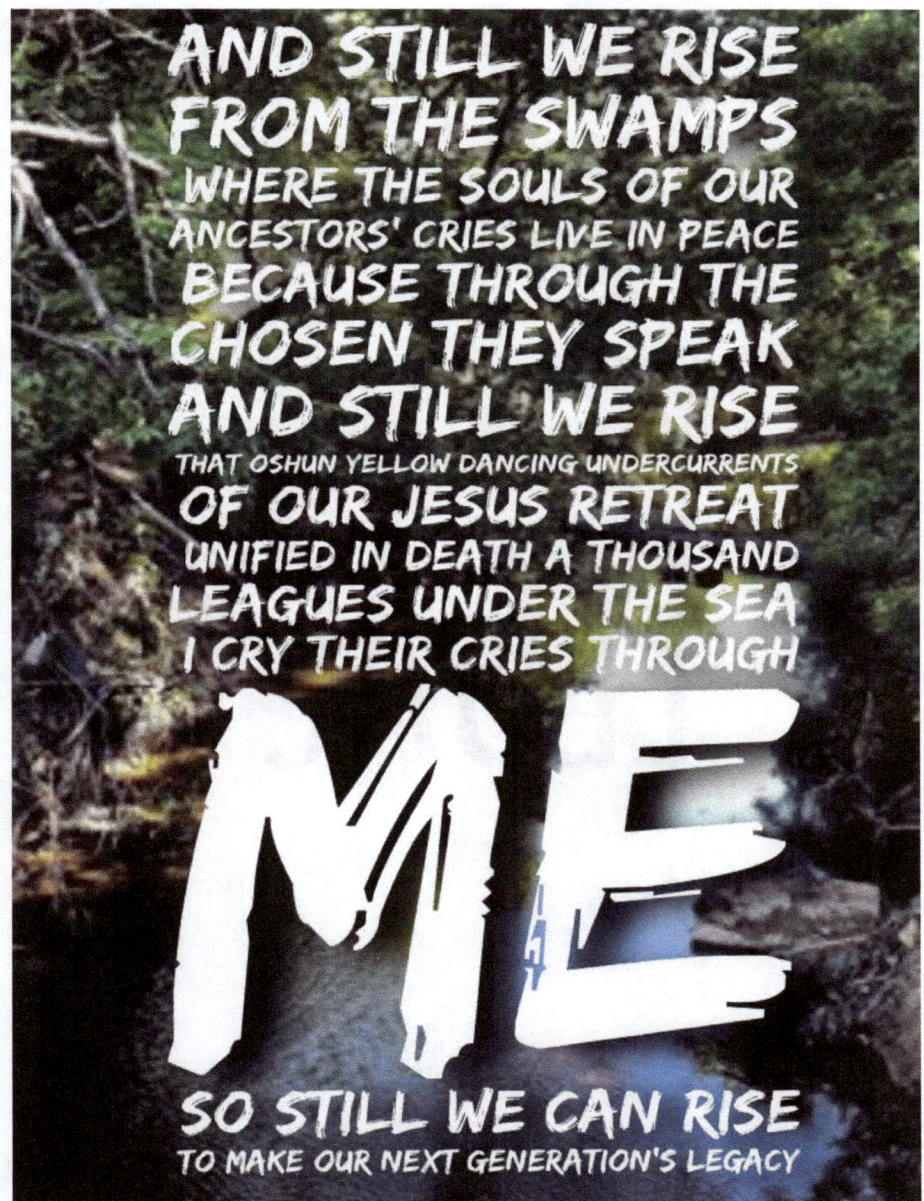

Janee Vaughn, June 10, 2020, *Solitude*, Photo session at Arlington parks in Texas, photograph

LEGACY

Is a legacy some books of poetry?
For some it can be.
My legacy is in how I live.
How my smile changes those I meet.
How my soul
Grabs a hold
And never leaves.
My legacy is in my babies.
How Jessie's voice carries you away in a tune,
Before you know it, bare feet are dancing shoes.
How the thought of her voice makes you think of a new song.
How Jordan embodies the meaning of what it is to be strong.
How she's always planning.
And learning something new,
Always saying yes to opportunities, she grew.
How Joey's respect for women and his elders

Leads by example for the younger ones he shelters.
How his strength in silence
And his masculine tones
Echo in his actions.
Because he knows that while words do have power
Movement really matters.
My legacy is the life I lead to inspire others to grow and to be
Whoever and whatever their hearts desire them to see...
The way I make others feel wanted and never alone.
How I'm always a call away by text or phone.
No matter how we may have ended
My legacy is about making new beginnings.
A chance to grow in a new season,
A chance to make life have a new meaning,

A chance to let your past go away,
A chance to master something new for '90 mins for 90 days',
Thank you K.B. Power for leading the way.
A chance to learn something about someone that grows you closer.
A chance to grow wiser so you can grow older.
A chance to become more than you could ever know.
Turning a like into a passion, so your talent can grow.
And not just being heard but being seen.
Reliving old childhood dreams.
My legacy is about becoming more than that teen
Lost in a system mazing a way through,
More than seeing a celly mating with some dude,

Becoming more than a number,
statistic, a "black" soul shot in the dark.
My legacy is about creating the last Black Ark.
Sparking that art
That sparks the spark.
So, we can hard reset Black Lives Matter
And get a new start,
Sovereignty from America.
Get back to our roots.
Build a wall of black art that covers US from U..(SA),
America the not so beautiful:
Land of homemade terrorists and apple pie lies.
A death ticket
In every birth certificate.
While they get 9 lives.
My legacy is about building

Generational wealth, not just making millions.
Growing wealthy in love of those surrounding you.
Becoming a millionaire from something simple,
Like LFLS did with a concept of a shoe.
Or
Deciding that this time, this is the last drink,
Last snort, last heroine shot, last smoke of that gas ass dank.
Deciding to be organically who you were born to be,
Not what society says,
But who you choose
Because you're free.
Free.
Free.
Yes, you are free...
Free, to make your own legacy!

Jasmine's Twilight

Perspectives are filtered by our life lessons and experiences.
We have to accept everyone can't stretch
imagination or thought processes to see,
we sometimes stunt our own progresses
by thinking we are all the same;
forgetting the beauty from whence we came.
We are all perfect and fearfully made.
I don't see hate. It's just a different hue, no shade.

Janee Vaughn, *Sunset Memorial,* Copperas Cove Lewisville Lake Texas session at sunset August 26, 2020, Photograph,

Jasmine's Twilight

No prophet shall bear false witness
Prophetic visions prevail on false reality television
Shows hands of faith
Persecution of the masses
Wrong turn
Reverse to self-refraction
Projection: an inability to see oneself reflected
Yet, pastors still mark on beasts
Dust to dust carbon copies
All praises be in a system
Amalgamated in Pontius' Pilot
Light turned on to Ishtar's Dynasty
Henged on Stones cloaked in secrecy
Foundations of mortar and brick masonry
Reworking works sufficiently
Filling nooks of mental deficiency
Books of false prophecies
Copies of natural resources
And elemental things
Earth, water, fire, wind, air of heirs
Impossibly composed on papyrus
Rewrote roles
Circle cog
Square hole
Still fulfilled
Missing links
In chains of faith
By which we should walk
When we were given full sight
Self-detoxifying third eye
Melanin restructuring collateral damage
Ancestral DNA
Meditate in faith
See with closed eyes
Sought faith passed down
Is how we got by
Bye bye, sheep heard-her
Oral tradition spoken in current times
Unwritten scriptures
Scripted in digital revision
Revising scripts
Rewritten by prophetic visions
Replayed by false reality television puppets
Of this injustice system

Numbers Do Know Boundaries

Sometimes numbers do know boundaries
Boundaries with numbers
Is a sketchy lottery
Like, which truth you hiding
To spread these lies to me
And what hate you fueling
When you know, obviously
All you spread on the news
That's lies too
SEE
We must've forgotten why we have T.V.
It was meant to train brains
To get on tracks with trains
That aim for them in mainstream
Stream all your cares away
Natural disaster
Becomes unnatural catastrophe

Jasmine's Twilight

A volcano erupting is conspiracy
Masquerades
A swarm of locusts
Is now our deadly fate
Yet, we've been dealing with these demons
For centuries
Now we're letting these demons take over we
We no longer have our own degrees
University we started
Now, lack of money bans us from university
But that's ok
It's no longer knowledge they teach
So, it's no longer knowledge we do speak
It's all just cowards
Learning to cower
SEE
We be bastards of illiteracy
We be movers and shakers
of *their movie industry*

Promoting the hate, we see in we
Promoting the indigenous hate of we
SEE
The one thing I can tell you
Out of anything else is
We left knowledge of world
And knowledge of self
For knowledge of wealth
Less spiritual health
Materialistic prompting
Of our spiritual deaths
We are birth
SEE
That be that original sin
Sun of man rising
Knowledge at birth descends
Into the depths of our recesses
Cortex left pressed
Instead of using what we were blessed
We use 10% or less
And wonder about
The hand we are dealt

Calcify all ties
Kill all self
Third eye unrevived
Your spiritual death
Natural phenomena we miss
Instead, we follow numbers of this
One world government
Mist veils eyes
We walk, not by sight
All the way blind
Not by faith
Of that we've been robbed
Straight off cliffs
Waiting for a messiah
We are the messiah
In plain clothes hiding
They held back powers
So, we can lose vision
Stake burned
Called us witches
Ancestors in realms
Beyond *their* own visions
Ancestors telling tales
Of now made industry
Making moves

They now use
To change you
To change our history
We are left unremembering
Who we are
What we should be
Hailing us
gods and goddesses
Refractions of light we
Need only a fraction more
To regain vision
Stand in unity
Minus division
Realize we are suns revived
Once we've arisen
We greet, 'Grand rising Kings and Queens'
Let's get this provision!

AREN'T WE ALL BORN IN SIN?
I SAY AGAIN
AREN'T WE ALL BORN IN SIN?
THE SIN AMERICA BORE US IN
WE WERE BORN
PERFECT REFLECTIONS OF A
GOD
YET WE SEEK OUTSIDE OF SELF
SAVING GRACE HAS BEEN
♥ • ♥ • ♥   BORN IN US   ♥ • ♥ • ♥
MELANIN ACTIVATES VITAMIN,
MINERALS
REPLENISHES EARTHLY PATTERNS
CREATION'S REFLECTIONS
BEYOND CLEAR VISION
WHY SEEK DIVISION OF A
✘ ✘ ✘ PERFECT SYSTEM? ✘ ✘ ✘

Jasmine's Twilight

Black Wombman Is GOD

My friend loves to tell me
how women are born unclean.

So, I ask...

How can women be born to sin
When my god has been given
Passageway for me to be born
Man, you ain't know
The black wombman is god

All man say is woman be scorn
Torn to pieces by worldly
heathens
Who don't respect
the life they're mistreating

Which created life of all races
We are one
Yet not all can sustain the sun
Man, you ain't know
The black wombman is god

Rising and falling
She be moon
Mood creator of any room,
Oshun
Kali, the center of his doom
Karmic recycler
Handing out returns of all form
The only hater who can touch you
Is the one _he_ has born
Man, you ain't know
The black wombman is god

Hate is taught
A concept by man
Who tells us to wash
Our unclean hands
Of the sin of life
So, we begin again
Religious circles
Trying to fit in
The black wombman is god
Respect her skin

gods and goddesses
Don't hold earthly realm
We walk on waters deep
Steering at the helm
Directing life flows
We create our own hell
How can we be unclean?

when my god is the swell
Of all current and passing
subsiding waves
She washes me clean
Has since early days
The black woman forgives
A savior in grace

She feeds my soul
In more than spiritual ways
She heals me
Comforts me
Protects my life from dark days
The torment I lived
Was all man made
So how can we be unclean
When from a god we were made
The black wombman is god

Jasmine's Twilight

Quell your lips when you speak her name

Respect to only pass through
She plays no games
Hips swaying
Pie baking
Teaching kids to behave
Caring for elders
Selfless acts of love
Knows no shame

The black wombman is god
No need to bow down
She is the reason
We learn to walk in faith
So next time you see a god
Treat her accordingly

PHARM
TO MARKET ROAD

For a hundred years
They said it was the gateway drug
Now they wanna be the dealer
Government control
Ain't never yield a healer
Death and sickness
For the sake of corporate riches
For a few dollars an hour we sell out
Like a bunch a bitches
Cure for cancer
They banned that shit
Kept it hidden
The truth about AIDS
Is they're the ones
That got it delivered
Why is there a patent
On our forms of sickness?
Heavy metals and poisons
They try to stick us
Vaccinate for your health
Nah, vaccinate for their wealth
The kingpin gotta stay in control
Ain't nobody stopping their money train
They're on a coal burning roll
Right over anyone that gets in their way
Judges, cops, even their own doctors they slay
They call us witches so we can be on a hunt list

Because we try to get you off this permanent sick shit
Then they poison the food and herbs that make you whole
There's even a patent on your soul
Snatch that quick
Then rob your pockets
But that's okay because
The sheeple just go with it
Eating away to earlier and earlier graves
Wilding about genders
Like we weren't taught how to behave
But it's what they put in the foods that keeps us their slaves
Go to Africa and you won't find the same things to eat
There you find preservative free veggies and meat
But what do I know?
I ain't nothing but a sheep
Now let me be quiet
Here they come
Let's pretend that we're still asleep

Soapbox

You know how it is
When another shade
Says the same thing you said
THEN... it's a good idea

Let's talk about it

Ain't no part of me insecure
Self-esteem's just fine
Matter fact, put me in any dark room
I'm liable to be the only thing that shine
Feed me to the wolves
I come out leading the line

The problem is most people are weak
Too scared to step out on faith
And walk in their purpose like me
Too afraid to be a freak

Let's talk about it

What's normal in a dysfunctional society

Jasmine's Twilight

You worrying about why he/she doin' shit
Can't even manifest ya own destined bliss

Keeping up with the Joneses
The Clarks chaining doors
Leaning on understanding
Of a future untold

Let's talk about it

Sold on the idea of inclusion
Like the slave masters and the Uncle
Ruckus' weren't in collusion
Marcus Garvey wanted you to be uprooted
Leave your Native land
And be slaves of a new suitor

Still painting me as the angry black woman
Run up on me, then call me aggressive
Try to take MY man, then call me possessive
Like I'm supposed to lay down and be submissive

Fuck all ah that shit!

Let's talk about it

We saw George Floyd die on film
That ain't stop police violence
That ain't get clean water for Flint
That ain't help us with the mentally challenged homeless

Who're kicked out of facilities to live on street corners
Persecuted because they have no supporters
No structure innate
So, they're literally bashed and murdered because of pure hate

Let's talk about it!

All these Proud Boys flailing flags of a losing team
Tryna reenact a change in their history
Surging their own structures
Talk about a function in dysfunction

That just don't make no sense

How you take down the system made for you
Literally, YOUR OWN government
Made to protect your inalienable right to be stupid
We all know it was an inside job at the capital
That's why we ain't see a lot of shooters

Let's talk about it

Microaggression to aggression per usual
Grocery stores, banks, corner stores, and schools too
It ain't never been comfortable in a black woman's shoes

Yet you can't wait to get laced
Fake asses and boobs in bustiers
Changing noses and lips
Now you can't tell me shit
With that paralysis on the left side of your face
Who told you to use poison to try to be another race?

That's like tryna change ya sex
It's all moot
You were perfectly made by God
Why can't you even love you?

Let's talk about it

America don't love nothing unless it's green
The sooner you see that
The sooner we can wipe the slate clean
Stand up and get the monopoly board off our backs
I'm talking real unity in numbers
Not just in theory
Actual stats

I know I started this off as a rant
That's exactly what it'll be
Until we can talk about the uncomfortable things
We will never end racism
And this will be an ongoing theme
and we 'gon keep talkin' 'bout it

Acknowledgements

Writing this book has taught me a lot. The most important thing I have taken away from this experience is the gratitude I have for every single person I have encountered on this journey. I am forever humbled by the talent I have been blessed to have surrounding me. The skills I learned came from those who helped me to be more resilient, self-reliant, confident, & most capable. I thank all of you who are reading this book. I hope it brings about a revolution in you, to grow in research and knowledge of how to be the best you. Thereby, you will be able to be a tool of change and a light of hope for all in your community.

Thank you for your support and genuine love!

Janeé Vaughn

About the Author

Janeé Vaughn is a spoken word artist from New Orleans, Louisiana. She resides in DFW - Dallas Fort Worth metroplex, Texas. She is a published writer, artist, chef, musician. This is her first self-published series of books, Jasmine's Twilight. She produces art shows to showcase multifaceted creatives, such as herself. She is 1/12 of TribeLifeNationProductions, a group of 12 artists like herself. She is ¼ of MPromptToo, an online writing group, created by Melissa Williams, set to continue to spark creative's inspiration. Janeé is the curator of TribeNubianWriters writing group. She created this space to facilitate a place for creatives to grow strength in short stories and script writing. Lastly, she is also a Deadly Pen, a fraternal order of the best international writers, headed by Gregg Delaney of The Colorado Commission. You can follow her on Instagram @browngoddess1979 and on Facebook as Jasmine Vaughn.

www.ingramcontent.com/pod-product-compliance
Lightning Source LLC
Chambersburg PA
CBHW050645160426
43194CB00010B/1817